Heart Gifts Make Memories of a Lifetime

By Cathy Brooks

This book is based on a real life story and a series of events. The hard work of two people from their native hometown of Waverly, Virginia, miraculously was reunited many years later to share knowledge of a heart gift from the towns' ice man.

Copyright © 2013 by Cathy Brooks
www.luvbearsedutainment.com

All rights reserved. No part of this book may be reproduced or transmitted in any form or by any means, electronic or mechanical, including photocopying, recording, or by any information storage and retrieval system, without written permission from the publisher.

Per Mrs. Shirley S. Yancey, Museum President for Miles B. Carpenter Museum, permission was granted for use of this information on November 3, 2012.

Disclaimer: Some names and characters have been changed in order to maintain the privacy of individuals.

Formatted by Cody Hopkins

Edited by Sheila G. Jefferson

ISBN: 978-0615974484

Dedication

This book is dedicated to those who believe in their vision, natural gifts and talents. In addition, they aspire to use their skills creating synergy helping themselves, as well as others in their community. Their wisdom to encourage others to find their uniqueness and their purpose to help them understand the courage it takes to make a difference.

Acknowledgements

First and foremost, my husband, Cornell and I would like to express our sincere gratitude to our beloved families and friends. Their encouragement, many blessings and continued support over the years has meant the world to us.

Secondly, we would also like to extend our gratitude to the amazing people who willingly shared their words of wisdom with us on our incredibly miraculous journey. We are truly grateful for the compassionate three wise elderly women for their guidance, by them standing firmly in the gap and giving so many encouraging messages of hope.

We are also grateful for all of the individuals, churches and organizations who have volunteered their time in so many capacities to help their community, especially the spouses that helped with preparation as they patiently waited at the events.

Additionally, we are very thankful for all of the beautiful children, parents, teachers and childcare centers that initially inspired us to keep moving forward. We appreciate your engagement in our pretend farm trip creating an on-site pop-up box farmhouse in the classrooms. We wish to thank the Richmond Public Library for our first opportunity to hit the stage with our Luv Bear Puppets and Life on the Farm with Penny Peanut Programs, and the many sponsors for their generosity and donations to support our presentation of the peanut heritage of Sussex County at the State Fair of Virginia. Our deepest appreciation goes out to First Baptist Church and the Miles B. Carpenter Museum for being a firm foundation in the community, and opening their doors to welcome us back home with our work, particularly for being instrumental in the delivery of our Book Swap and Can-Do Kids Programs. This supported our effort to help children build their home library increasing awareness of the importance of early learning for future success in school.

Our special thanks also goes out to the Director of Services at the Book Bank for her help in redirection on resuming our work in which came forth the new Literacy Arts Program and Book Swap, and to everyone that sincerely dedicated their hearts, devoted their time and hosting our programs over the years.

This book could not have been possible without the support of the many heroes and she-roes, who taught us the art of resilience from their own journey. The successful outcome of this dream idea project became a reality for everyone by continuing to believe in the vision, as well as the spirit of teamwork and the encouragement from others to never give up hope.

Table of Contents

Heart Gifts Make Memories of a Lifetime i

Dedication iii

Acknowledgements v

Introduction 3

Two Little Peanut Girls Teamwork - Past - Present - Future 5

Mothers and Mentors Women of Wisdom - Mothers of Multiple Skills 11

An Interview with Mrs. Shirley S. Yancey 15

Mrs. Shirley S. Yancey First Miles B. Carpenter Museum Volunteer Director of 28 Years 16

The Founding of Miles B. Carpenter Museum 18

Birth of the Nation's First Peanut Museum in U.S.A 20

Returning Home Riding Down Peanut Country Road 22

The Gift Shop and Community Welcome Invitation 24

Life Lessons Learned From the Farm 26

The Art of Remaining Resilient 29

Mentors Planting Seeds through Words of Wisdom 31

The Birth of Penny Peanut 33

Penny Peanut's New Message of Hope 39

Faith and Courage 41

People that are put in Your Pathway 47

Promoting the Peanut Heritage at the State Fair of Virginia 50

Historic 200 Pound Watermelon Story 52

Cherry Blossom Trees and the Volunteer Appreciation Ice Cream Social 54

Peanut Harvest Time November 2, 2013 Return Home to Visit 57

A Special Thank You to
Miles B. Carpenter Museum 60

Introduction

"None of us got where we are solely by pulling ourselves up by our bootstraps. We got there because somebody – a parent, a teacher, an Ivy League crony or a few nuns – bent down and helped us pick up our boots."– Thurgood Marshall

This book is an encouragement for those who seek to chase their dreams and heartfelt passion, also to help place value on the importance of volunteering as you leave a trail of little heart gifts along the way while helping others, as well as gaining knowledge, skills and experiences for future work. In this particular case, it gave hope to a dream that became reality despite the challenges. It was inspired through the spirit of teamwork between two people from their native town. They were reunited years later and volunteered at a community event. It is intended to be used as a resource tool to encourage the support of volunteers and to bring an increase in awareness to the importance of community involvement. They believed that their ideas and dreams became reality through their spirit of teamwork. This helped everyone involved reap the benefits of a lifetime championship.

The book you hold in your hands contains a series of events that took place over a period of fifteen years which created a life of its own. In addition, it is to help gain insight and knowledge of their passionate work and its purpose. Upon the two reuniting, they agreed to try to find ways to help share knowledge about a longtime resident that they both knew. Their desire was to support his request of the heart gift that he left behind for his community.

They envisioned ways of how they could help each other through their work to expand the knowledge of the beautiful historical landmarks in and beyond their hometown. Their plan was to share knowledge of the legacy of Miles B. Carpenter, a nationally known Folk Artist, along with his collection of Primitive Folk Art. Additionally, a part of the plan was to help increase awareness of the peanut heritage surrounding Sussex County in Waverly, Virginia and the Nation's First Peanut Museum in U.S.A. Together, they created the enthusiasm and strength needed to provide resource tools in order to expand the peanut history beyond their hometown.

At this point, there might be a question or two. How did an artist from the region get the opportunity to share this remarkable story from afar? It is amazing how our acceptance to a "welcome back home invitation" to volunteer led to starting it all. Displaying at this central facility allowed us to work with local children and their families throughout the community.

In the midst of it all, it is my hope that everyone will have a greater understanding about this as they gain knowledge of the beautiful historical landmark's origin. It is my pleasure to present the story of the two little peanut girls. Amazing things began to unfold as they held on to their courage to pursue their work of the legacy of the heart gift left behind.

Two Little Peanut Girls
Teamwork - Past - Present - Future

Spirit of teamwork

Have you ever wondered about the possibility of your dream idea and how it may emerge? Do you have what it takes to stay focused and put forth the effort to make it happen? Over the years, a lot of wise people have come into my pathway and have spoken words of wisdom into my life. Along the way they've all left a trail of little heart gifts behind.

One stands out in particular; a few years ago a wise elderly woman shared a new poem with me to add to my inspirational list of Do It Anyway Poem collections. She asked me to take a few moments to read one of her favorites titled "Drinking from My Saucer." Collectively, after reading the poem, the message was so inspirational; they led me to move forward.

At this point in time, our pathways have gone in different directions with our future work. So many wonderful people have joined us along this incredible journey. After taking a closer look, I began to take note of a few questions. Which program would be a storehouse to preserve the wise powerful words of wisdom that left behind a trail of little heart gifts of a lifetime? Who were and still are those beautiful flowers planted in my Garden of Life? Then the green light flashed on with a new dream idea! Fortunately, as we moved forward, our M&M WOW-MOMS TEAM was just waiting at the crossroads of my life to emerge. This program is where we are paying tribute and preserving all of the powerful words of wisdom to support future learning. What's so good about it is that, as we worked together, she always embraced the spirit of teamwork. The perception of the message was that it is through faith, believing in your dreams while helping others grow, along with the spirit of teamwork is what yields championships.

For example, this might be a scenario that many people may have encountered. You spend many years investing your time with a company while observing their difficult daily challenges. Your ultimate dream desire is to remain stable in hope for potential growth without a job change. In an attempt to show interest in the future of the company, you suggest a new workshop idea. This will increase productivity, offer resource tools and help the staff improve in their professional development.

The first company allows you to make a presentation. Afterwards, John, the Director approaches and gives you his feedback that the idea is unique and creative. He agrees to support you in the spirit of teamwork with your plans. Later, he invites you on board as a test pilot, but only through *volunteering* your services without any potential growth. Why not take a chance as this could possibly offer a brighter future and everyone can yield the championship? It seems like a good plan and will definitely improve the work environment. You do it anyway, then later see that you are just hanging out and going nowhere with your test pilot idea. So you move on to another job, but still believe in your dream idea never giving up.

Fortunately, at the new job you get a second chance to present your ideas. This time, the door widely opens with a few changes in direction. Maybe by chance, this time you can meet your family's needs, and grow with the company. This could be another scenario as well for many people.

For instance, you are in your classroom and Liz the Administrator walks in out of curiosity for a brief visit. She observes the children, their parents and the staff interacting in a fun array of on-site activities. You share the idea wanting to implement this new innovative method. It has already been effective in reaching parents, caregivers and children daily. Afterwards, she states that she is thrilled by her observation, feels that it is exquisite and that you should take off running.

First, she agrees to support the idea only on a *volunteer* basis. Secondly, she advises you not to try to reinvent the wheel just give it a new realignment. Then later informs you that her budget will not allow you a salary increase. On the other hand, she will recognize your work as a part of a "cultural enrichment" program. This would be for the sole purpose of enhancing the activities in the classroom environment.

Now the moment of truth has come. Your heart leads you to *volunteer* (yet again!) and do it anyway. Again, you will not get a salary increase or grow in your current position. With the help of your assistant, you offer this service to the community through your classrooms. Everyone is elated and benefits from the convenience of having on-site theme base interactive activities.

On the positive side of things, Liz kindly recognizes your credentials and experience with a Certificate of Excellence Award. Unfortunately, for everyone as the future requests for the program excels, it suddenly comes to a halt. Later she meets with you stating that the company will have to make budget cuts and is going in a different direction.

These two scenarios became my reality after spending years of trying to seek potential growth within the companies. In reflecting back at the brighter side of things, we are grateful for that phenomenal experience which evolved our programs through years of volunteering. Surprisingly, this all started after a sudden rain storm caused our planned family classroom event to be moved indoors. Now that we were all faced with a major dilemma for activities, I suggested that my co-workers carry on. It's still somewhat unbelievable, but as I searched for a quick fix, I stumbled upon a huge cardboard box waiting to be crushed.

Instantly, my thought was that this box could save the day and it became my new idea. It could also probably bring calm to the chaos created by the storm. Naturally, with a few moments of thinking outside of the box, the green light flashed bringing forth the birth of our pop-up on-site classroom program.

With a little creativity, some strong tape, and adding a few items for interactive play, I had created a huge farm box playhouse. The goal was to have the parents and their children go on a pretend trip to the farm. They were to learn about life on the farm. The excitement came when they played the counting game with the pop-up bear puppets in the woods.

In moving forward, with the loving support of my husband Cornell, we synchronized our talents creating large cardboard box theme based programs. A variety of music and dance was included to help make learning fun for the children, parents, and other caregivers. It is better known as Edutainment, which is a combination of entertainment and education. Edutainment is an effective way to help children learn by making the process fun with the engagement of activities. To this day, we are still amazed at how a sudden rain storm and a huge cardboard box could result in so many blessings. After taking a few moments to focus on redirection, the reality kicked in on the future potential benefits of the program. We desired to continue our work helping other children and their families spend quality time learning together in their daily lives. Part of the community outreach included programs that helped the children to recognize the elderly in nursing homes. This was done by making special ornaments to help share in their joy of learning.

This was a remarkable experience and my first dream idea that we believed in as we shared our heart gift of volunteering. For sure, both places supported the idea in the spirit of teamwork, but neither one met our request to help provide the needs of our family. Although we all went our separate ways, the life lessons learned helped us truly see the benefits of our work in the lives of the children.

Fortunately, this was a golden opportunity for us to work with so many families in their classrooms. It was a very positive experience and the blessings that overflowed were the most rewarding of all. They showed their appreciation and gratitude in so many ways while capturing priceless memories of a lifetime. Taking a closer look at the final end, we all yielded the championship. These experiences did not discourage us in any way to discontinue volunteering. They helped us gain advanced skills and knowledge to use in the future development of teaching children to be lifelong learners.

Our primary focus to continue this program resulted from us having to utilize the services of many centers over the years. While entering the classrooms, the most important thing that we searched for was the star teacher that shined the brightest. We observed her techniques, use of her skills and her interaction with the children and their families.

Often at times, we are faced with challenges that only empower us to move forward. There are many ways to look at the situation, but we are elated to have had a chance to initiate our footprint in the community. While still believing in the vision, we took our huge cardboard box idea with the pop-up mobile on-site classroom and started the ball rolling. Our thought was, "Why not pitch the idea to other childcare centers, libraries and organizations?" In an interesting way, things started to quickly turn around for us. The blessings began to flow after it became a business and our next job. Incredible things began to happen as we traveled some very bumpy roads with a few flat tires along the way.

Over the years many other doors continued to open that referred us for future presentations with rewarding sponsorships. We continued to still volunteer in the community as well as the nursing homes. This was especially true in the case of the museum. In the meantime, we presented what we thought was our farewell tour of fifteen years back in my hometown. This took place at the Miles B. Carpenter Museum with our Penny Peanut teaching toolbox character on November 3, 2012 at the Peanut Harvest Festival.

As the story began to unfold, this leads back to the beginning about the wise elderly woman and the two poems. We added Our Mothers and Mentors Team which was inspired by some very special people in our Garden of Life. In this particular case, it was the three wise elderly women that were waiting back home for my weekend visit. This program is intended to honor, pay tribute and celebrate their words of wisdom and guidance. Their message of hope is to celebrate the gift of life every day; be encouraged, stay focused, and through it all you will understand and find your purpose. In doing so, it will help you realize that in this life the seasons will unexpectedly change sometimes bringing you turmoil.

We must keep the faith and have the courage to get up and try again. The words that best describe the experience and the phenomenal moment, that I am about to share with you are truly wisdom, knowledge, encouragement and understanding.

Mothers and Mentors
Women of Wisdom -Mothers of Multiple Skills

There are many that come into our pathways that are like trees planted firmly, sincerely standing boldly and bravely through life's storms. Their roots have grown deeply and embedded into our ground. They continue to be a blessing, planting seeds of hope in others during their season. Through their vision and encouragement, their seeds of hope sown will produce a mighty forest someday, with many trees that will become richly filled with fruit, reaping a great harvest to help others. M&M WOW-MOMS

The New Year arrived, ringing in changes while we were getting acclimated to the work studio. We put our idea into action to bring in another teaching toolbox character to continue spreading the message of hope in the community. After settling down, we were once again invited to the Miles B. Carpenter Museum, to *volunteer* our services. We respectfully agreed, only this time the event was different. It was one of simplicity, where we captured astonishing memories to preserve as it all unfolded.

While waiting and enjoying the warm, gentle spring breeze, I observed with heartfelt compassion, savoring the moment as my mentor, Mrs. Shirley S. Yancey, gradually approached the guests to speak. She gave a remarkable recognition speech offering many words of wisdom at the Volunteer Appreciation Ice Cream Social. Afterwards, she invited the guests to gather around to enjoy their favorite ice cream sundae. Also, visit a small collection of memoirs of museum events featuring our work together. After greeting several guests, we held onto each other while we slowly walked down the hill for some much needed rest. Finally, we made it, as this was our favorite place to display our presentations. This was the first time that she could actually make the trip down the long hill to visit.

Many wise elderly women have crossed my pathway. They are blessings and are flowers that have been planted in my Garden of Life. By the way, this one in particular has an eclectic style with a wide range to reach people in her work. Allow me to unveil to you the wise elderly woman that I spoke about at the beginning of the story. She kindly shared her Drinking from My Saucer Poem to add to my Do It Anyway Poem collection. In an effort to help keep the vision moving forward, she has agreed to be a part of our M&M WOW-MOMS TEAM. It is time that I share with you, how I sat down as I embraced the very warm spring afternoon on April 7, 2013 in the Cedar Building on the grounds of the Miles B. Carpenter Museum. As I spoke with Mrs. Yancey, she immediately reminded me of the many priceless memories that we shared over the years.

Meanwhile, the spring breeze was blowing and all too consuming as the cherry blossom leaves calmly flowed through the air. We talked about how we were reunited and our journeys were since the first day fifteen years ago. The serenity that surrounded the grounds was calming as we watched videos that were captured of our passionate work.

Later, a few other people came by to enjoy the little treasures of collection of children events. I took a few minutes to step away to reflect back, as I envisioned many special moments while standing overlooking the beautiful grounds. I've observed her and many other dedicated volunteers give countless hours of their time to the museum. I met Mrs. Yancey in my childhood years. This was during the time that I attended school as the transitional stages of integration of Sussex County Schools took place. She was a substitute teacher that taught frequently and one of my many teachers that I would always look forward to seeing in school.

For years, she came into the classroom with a burst of energy always ready to teach us, making sure that we understood the importance of being in school. In general, I remember her instantly redirecting all of her students with her encouraging words. She would tell us to make good choices, stay in school and always keep learning. After a few minutes and with the late evening rapidly approaching, I returned to join them. We headed back up the long hill and said our goodbyes. We agreed to meet later to capture a series of events and plans to continue our work together.

Shortly after, this event we talked about our future and how our company could create another character. This was done to help deliver the messages to the children that we serve. In this case, she joined us through our teaching toolbox characters. This sparked our new teaching toolbox, the birth of Mrs. Y, who was created in acknowledgement of her and her work at Luv Bears Village Studios. Mrs. Y's character was created, assigned job duties and is the other little peanut girl in the story. She is now a part of our new M&M WOW–MOMS TEAM (Mothers and Mentors with Words of Wisdom). She along with the other two wise elderly women is one of our many mentors, that we have had the pleasure of having come in our pathway. They are all flowers in our Garden of Life that brings a wealth of knowledge and many powerful lessons through their journey.

Since that time, Mr. Roane, the current Museum Administrator has been appointed and once again, we were warmly welcomed to the community. We returned on November 2, 2013 with Penny Peanut and Mrs. Y to present a storyline at the Peanut Harvest Time. The most rewarding moment came as the real life Mrs. Y (Mrs. Shirley S. Yancey) made an appearance. She showed her support and offered a few words of wisdom for our Can-Do Kids Program. Many of our longtime attendees greeted us as they enjoyed the positive message of hope that she delivered. She encouraged children to stay in school and always want to learn more and more. Amazing things has happened as they continue to visit many children sharing their positive messages of hope and poems.

An Interview with Mrs. Shirley S. Yancey

In pursing this matter further, I asked Mrs. Yancey if she would share her wisdom and knowledge. This would also give me insight on herself and the origin of the Miles B. Carpenter Museum's history.

While doing my research, I discovered an exciting thing that relates to our story of the two little peanut girls and our work over the past fifteen years. She served two terms as president in The Woman's Club of Waverly and helped organize the Waverly Rescue Squad. During her second term, one theme that caught my attention under her leadership was My Community and Me. The discovery of this information alone exemplified our work together. I was elated that we could seize this moment in time to share this important information. It was my pleasure to interview a true historian with an incredible wealth of knowledge.

Mrs. Shirley S. Yancey First Miles B. Carpenter Museum Volunteer Director of 28 Years

Her Words of Wisdom

Returning a few weeks later we started the interview process while traveling through the area. During that time, we spent many hours together sharing information while taking a few quiet moments to listen to the sweet sounds of nature. After sitting back and stretching in her chair, I began with the first question of my interview, asking her what was her reason for this project and why she was so interested in peanuts. From this point, she simply smiled as she gave me a big chuckle.

She took me down memory lane in her very own words. She exclaimed, using her famous quote, "Well, my dear! Where do you want me to start? As it all happened, it all started right here in Sussex County. I am a lifetime resident of Waverly, Virginia and I was born during the Great Depression. I have been volunteering as the Museum Director for the Miles B. Carpenter Museum for the past 28 years.

My love for peanuts has been one from my childhood. I was raised on a peanut farm. During the 1930's and 40's, my father harvested peanuts to help support our family. Peanuts were very valuable to us as they helped us get through difficult times during the Great Depression. Every year during fall harvest, soon after all of the peanuts had been shucked my mother would take me outside. We would work as we gathered up all of the remaining peanuts that were left on the ground. We would take burlap bags along with us and pick one hundred pounds of peanuts and later sold them. We would get at least $10.00 for each bag. This gave me enough money to buy my school clothes and had a little left over to save for the future."

To me, the story became more intriguing and sparked increasing interest as we continued our conversation. Indeed, I was even more eager in my quest to gain additional knowledge about the origin of the museum. After taking a long overdue break, I asked her how she got involved with the Miles B. Carpenter Museum. Beneath it all, her face became instantly showered by her smile. I immediately noticed her heartfelt compassion as she was overcome by joy. Gradually, she spoke slowly as her voice began to quiver while reflecting back to that moment in time.

The Founding of Miles B. Carpenter Museum

She said calmly, "Upon the passing of Miles B. Carpenter in 1985, I went to his home to pay my respect to the family. I took a sweet potato pie and a rough draft of The Woman's Club of Waverly history book that we were in the process of having published. I carried the rough draft to show his son what his father had written about his mother, who was a member of The Woman's Club of Waverly. His son approached me about the property saying, "Shirley maybe you are the one that I need to talk to." He stated that his father had offered his property to the Town of Waverly so that the property could be used for everyone to enjoy.

The Town of Waverly did not accept the property, because they did not feel that they could afford to take on the financial responsibility. I told him that I would have to take the matter to the board. I went forward in doing so and The Woman's Club of Waverly inherited the home and property. They turned it into a museum recognizing the legacy of Miles B. Carpenter who was a nationally known folk artist (wood carver). The museum displays tools and carvings of Miles B. Carpenter's work. Galleries and exhibits were added to help encourage the work of young artists in the region.

We had very limited funds as we started the museum, with a budget of only $200.00. We set out to renovate the home as well as the workshop. People in the community also joined in to help us working diligently to restore the property.

The walls were stripped of the damaged wallpaper and were replaced to enhance the new image. Several wood carvings and paintings of his work were left behind that could be seen throughout the home. As of today, his legacy of Primitive Folk Art is scattered in museums and private homes across the country. Exhibit cases were obtained to display regional art exhibits. After spending countless hours, The Miles B. Carpenter home opened their doors as a museum on Memorial Day Weekend in 1986.

Currently, the Museum serves as a central facility for the arts by promoting educational, cultural, and charitable interest and preservation of historical heritage. The Miles B. Carpenter Museum Complex is registered with the Virginia Historic Landmarks Commission, the National Register of Historic Places and is A National Folk Art Site."

Birth of the Nation's First Peanut Museum in U.S.A

Over a period of time, we finally met to complete the interview. In doing so, I asked Mrs. Yancey about the birth of the Nation's First Peanut Museum in U.S.A and its origin.

While sitting back in her chair smiling, she said, "As we moved forward with the Miles B. Carpenter Museum, we realized that our peanut information should have a home aside from the Folk Art in the museum. Peanuts were an important part of Miles B. Carpenter's life. Our peanut information was stored outside on the back porch, which should have been in an area geared towards the history of peanuts.

After discussing the matter among The Woman's Club of Waverly members, some showed great interest in this project. We later decided to have the abandoned coal shed that was in the back of the house cleaned out. This was the birth of the Peanut Museum that was designed for educational purposes.

It was established in an effort to preserve and interpret our Sussex County Heritage of peanuts. Pictures and items in various forms were displayed to help visitors gain knowledge about peanuts, as well as the harvesting process. The First Peanut Museum opened its' doors on May 12, 1990 at the Miles B. Carpenter Museum Complex. It was later discovered that this was the nation's only museum that housed this type of artifacts, thus the beginning of a Peanut Museum. Upon learning there was no peanut museum at that time, the museum was named the First Peanut Museum in U.S.A. Over the past 28 years, it has been our dream to help the community preserve our longtime resident and town's ice man legacy."

All of us are all left with fond memories of Mr. Carpenter, his work and his Chevrolet Truck from which he displayed and sold many of his carvings. Today his legacy still stands in the community and is a beautiful historical landmark for everyone to enjoy. With this in mind, I told her that she was a true historian with a great sense of humor and an awesome teacher. She chuckled again saying, "Well my dear! That is how the story unfolded."

We ended our day with a warm embrace and said our goodbyes. In conclusion, we reflected back at our reunion in 1998, as we both got a big chuckle while remembering the dangerous walk across the busy 460 highway.

Returning Home Riding Down Peanut Country Road

Priceless treasures

At this point I simply asked myself a question. How did the two little peanut girls end up together again? Subsequently, this sparked a few thoughts about returning home. What happened when Mrs. Yancey crossed that busy 460 Highway to welcome us to the community? Aside from that, the wooded nature reminded me of the priceless memories of the life lessons that my grandfather, Grandpa Claude, taught us while visiting him on the farm.

I took a few moments to travel down memory lane on that breezy fall day in October 1998. The peaceful nature was tranquilizing while I sat quietly gazing out of the window as my husband, Cornell, drove down Route 460. The air was filled with gusty winds blowing as colorful leaves fell all around the long stretch of peanut country highway. Immediately, memories of my life living there were quite evident. Just the excitement of being closer to my family and setting up a mini gift shop was a true blessing. It was my passion for inspirational art and planting seeds of hope that led me to return to my native hometown to work.

As we drove closer to town, I took a moment to embrace that special and familiar place that left a lifetime of heart prints deeply embedded within me. It was a rural town that I've cherished along life's journey, never forgetting the little peanut girl that grew up there. This is where so many words of wisdom flowed through my ears. They helped me truly understand who, what and where to place value in order to be successful on my journey.

Somewhere in the midst of it all, this was the very

beginning of an extended work relationship. It paved many roads to our future programs with the local children in the community. Nevertheless, this was not a claim to fame neither was it glamorous. It was one that was richly filled with love, and a tremendous lifetime of lessons from some very wise people.

The Gift Shop and Community Welcome Invitation

Give a little heart gift of a lifetime

Cornell and I were in the process of opening our new inspirational Art and Craft Gift Shop. Our hope was that we could share a few homemade gifts made from the heart. While traveling down the highway into town we attracted the attention of many people as we parked our Winnebago RV. It was loaded with boxes of items uniquely handcrafted and ready to stock the shelves. The shop was located off of the busy Route 460 Highway directly across from the Miles B. Carpenter Museum. We knew that this was an area that was well traveled where tourists could stop in on their way to the beach. In doing so, perhaps they could pick up a small treasure to take with them as well as visit the museum.

While pulling items out of the boxes, unpacking and trying to get set up; I took a moment to pause while taking a quick glance out of the window to enjoy the beautiful fall scenery. Surprisingly, across the busy 460 Highway, I saw a very familiar face from my past. It was Museum Director Mrs. Yancey coming by to welcome us back home.

She, along with many other wonderful teachers stood firmly in the gap for me during my years in school. As the years went by, I was consistently faced with a few daily challenges of my left-handed penmanship. It became a rewarding experience as I learned to master the art of adapting to the right-handed dominant world that surrounded me daily. This only gave me the courage and desire for learning even more in order to cope with the difficulties. With encouragement from my family, it was at this early stage that I discovered my passion for art by creating little heart gifts for people. We embraced each other while sharing many wonderful memories of our school years.

She stated that she came by to welcome us to the community and to offer an invitation to volunteer our services at the Peanut Harvest Festival on November 7, 1998. While doing so, she mentioned that this was an opportunity to invite the community and establishments to get involved to help support the museum. In other words, she wanted us to do one little simple thing that would make a difference. Namely, in this case the approach was different, very sincere and heartfelt.

Being that we had already volunteered our services in our church, jobs and community, we gladly agreed to return giving our support. Because of our acceptance to help at this event, many opportunities have risen for all of us. As a result, many benefits came as it increased awareness of the legacy of Miles B. Carpenter, the peanut heritage of Sussex County and the Nation's First Peanut Museum in U.S.A.

It was this invitation that has allowed us to expand and educate others for years living in and out of town. We chatted about our interests and how we could help each other through our work.

Life Lessons Learned From the Farm

It all starts right at home

Eventually, I did get a chance to reflect back and zone in on some of the priceless memories. They were captured as we frequently visited Grandpa Claude on the farm where he lived and worked. Furthermore, this is where our family, our very first teachers, planted seeds of hope in our early lives. As for me, several wise people taught me many survival skills through my resilient foundation, especially our grandfather.

I was born on a farm where he lived as a tenant farmer. Although our family relocated to another area in town, we spent a lot of time around our grandparents. One of my most treasured memories and appreciation for the rural scenic nature came as his grandchildren followed him around freely playing on the farm. He was one that was deeply loved, admired and respected for his great quality of integrity and tenacity. Born in the late 1800's, he later became a veteran in the U.S. Army enlisting on August 5, 1918, serving his country in the First World War. This was a historical moment that impacted many families.

Seriously, take a moment to just think about the enormous amount of strength that it took for a man of his character, to remain resilient in the era in which he lived through all of the challenges. Remarkably, he came back home from the war to his family, started life all over again with limited work skills, education and financial support. He was a very caring, energetic and determined gentleman who was always going about his business taking care of his family. Knowing how to maintain order among us, he used his work as teachable moments to help us learn good work ethics and the value of integrity.

Being around Grandpa Claude and observing his life as a farmer has helped me to truly understand the importance of learning how to use your natural gifts and talents to become self-sufficient while helping others along the way. It also increased awareness of local community based agriculture and its benefits. We watched him excel as he overcame many obstacles through his farm lifestyle and his work over the years. It was truly unbelievable how he learned to master the skills and techniques that he had, using them to the best of his ability to get the job done. This baffled us at times as he talked to us about his job while we ran along beside him playing and simply being children.

All along, he was preparing and teaching his grandchildren ways to reap the benefits of a great harvest, and we simply thought that he was just playing silly games with us. The wise valuable lessons that he taught us are priceless. Despite the fact that he had to adapt to so many challenges, his heart never altered away from the immense outpouring of love that he had for his family. His grandchildren would all get together spending countless nights just simply having a blast on the farm. We were always curious in our discoveries as we often got lost in the wooded nature that surrounded us while running and playing, creating our own games. One of the most interesting things about going to see him was the ride down the long country winding lane. Our faces were bursting with smiles as the car slowly approached the house. We eagerly jumped out, running and holding up our little arms to greet him. In his early years, looking straight up at him from the viewpoint of a child's eyes, he was our strong tall hero. It was a fact that we were almost guaranteed that he would be standing on the front porch at the door. Always smiling, waiting as he gently reached down, lifting each one of us up and playing airplane lifts.

Spending nights on the farm was filled with excitement as we barely got a good night's sleep knowing what we had to look forward to the next morning. Awakened by the early morning sun shining in our faces, everyone anxiously jumped out of bed and got dressed without hesitation to help him with his work. Then we all ran downstairs outside for Grandpa Claude to take us for a ride on the back hitch of the tractor. The ride was mesmerizing as we all laughed while sliding around falling on each other when the tractor hit the bumps in the road. We held our hands out to hold our clothes down as the wind blew through them while enjoying the fresh smell of apples and peaches sifting through the air. When the tractor stopped, we jumped off running, freely playing and hiding from each other. Shortly afterwards, we ran under our favorite tree and gathered up as many apples and peaches as we could that had fallen on the ground. Later, we all would get together and picked as many peanuts as we could find that were left in the fields after harvesting.

After a while, we caught up with our grandpa and followed him around the farm. That is what sparked my interest and eagerness to learn more about living on the farm and what he did to survive that incredible life. Meanwhile, he was also teaching and showing us the techniques as we did not know that he was preparing us for a life of future learning.

The Art of Remaining Resilient

Planting seeds for the future

It is such experiences as these that have allowed me to truly understand the art of remaining resilient and appreciate all of the heroes and she-roes. One of the most remarkable facts about Grandpa Claude's job was we observed his loyal dedication to the daily tasks that were never ending. He did not have access to the modern day equipment or tools that would help expedite the process, or make his work load much easier, as it is today.

As the years went by, we continued to see his challenges and realized that the work was very physical with extensive amounts of manual labor. Despite the many accidents that he had on the farm and the obstacles that came along, he always remained resilient, never giving up.

All the while, we continued to help out and it seemed as if the more ground we covered it took forever to finish the job. It was remarkable and unbelievable to us, the things that he had to get done daily to maintain the farm and take care of his family. We would often see him at times out in the family garden.

Some of us gathered tools to help him with his work. He showed us the proper way to dig holes and how to plant seeds. Then we would follow him around with our little buckets while he taught us how to pick the vegetables and fruit. Our strong tall hero never gave up despite his tiredness as he was always determined to keep going using every opportunity to teach us what he knew about life on the farm.

As young children, we did not understand what was happening to him as we watched his health slowly decline. Eventually, the time came years later when things began to unravel with his age and he rapidly began to slow down. In brief, looking forward to seeing him standing on the porch waiting to play airplane lifts with us came to a screeching halt. No more rides on the back hitch of the tractor, following him around the farm, or him teaching us how to plant seeds in the garden.

In brief, we watched as our strong tall hero transformed into a gentle, frail, gray haired, elderly man that could barely move around. As we continued to visit, he was often found sitting in his favorite chair on the front porch. In any case, we still jumped out of the car with our little hands in the air running as our hearts filled with joy to give him a great big hug. All things considered, our visits found him still continuously working taking care of his family.

The only thing different each time, was that he would be sitting using his hands often preparing vegetables and fruits from the garden. Some of us would join him to help out as we sat around listening to his favorite stories of all time.

The moment finally came when he put our skills to the test to show him what we had learned from his wise teachings. He was no longer mobile enough to go out to work in the garden. So he asked us to go instead, to replenish the tubs and pick more vegetables and fruit. The greatest reward was that even though he was playing silly games with us we were learning and watching him closely, gaining skills all along.

He was always encouraging us to stay focused on the task at hand, even if it was challenging and never giving up was the one thing that he stood firm on. He taught us to always take the time to do the necessary work in order that we may become self-sufficient. And in doing so, that the final results one day would be a great harvest that we all would be able to reap the benefits and help others.

Mentors Planting Seeds through Words of Wisdom

It starts at birth

"Every child has the potential to do great things in life, just give them a chance to shine their light."

-- Cathy Brooks

Our grandpa was so focused on what he had to do as he had mastered the art of farming so well, it was just second nature to him. He would proudly get up every day regardless of his situation and start to work as if he was going to a fancy office job on Wall Street. The reality kicked in over the years as we observed his dedication. As I reflect back on the experience, I can only appreciate the foundation that they all laid ahead for us in our lives to help pave the roads to our future. In essence, he was a great mentor and an awesome teacher that always poured words of wisdom into us as he knew what he was doing and could always bounce right back. After leaving home to pursue my future plans, I found myself on a return visit two weeks later.

Sadly, his health continued to decline and life took a turn for all of us as we all were deeply heartbroken by his departure in September 1975. He left behind many priceless heart gifts of a lifetime for future generations yet to come. Furthermore, it was that daily life of simplicity that has allowed me to foster my God given gifts, talents and creativity from his teachings.

Fortunately, for all of us, he returned home with the courage to fight even harder for the sake of his family, never giving up hope. We are truly honored and grateful for our strong tall hero. He will be remembered most of all for his great quality of integrity and tenacity along with his wise lifetime teachings.

Therefore, I am paying tribute to honor his courage for serving his country and powerful words of wisdom with this program to his family, as well as his grandchildren that have served their country. In moving forward with my work, I reflected back on how he handled surviving the First World War. My inspiration to create Penny Peanut's teaching toolbox character came from my real life experiences on the farm, to always believe in the vision and continue to plant seeds of hope despite the challenges. Her storyline was created after being invited to the library for a special presentation. This idea came about in an effort to promote the importance of early learning together to a diverse group of urban city preschoolers about life on the farm.

The Birth of Penny Peanut

Be spontaneous

"You can design and create, and build the most wonderful place in the world. But it takes people to make the dream a reality." --Walt Disney

It has been said that three strikes you are out of the game. But in this particular case, we just had to keep it moving forward. After continuing to volunteer my program in the classroom as an outreach to the community, I received our first invitation to the Richmond Public Library in 2006 to present a spring story time program with our bear puppets. They presented a storyline where they lived and played in the woods behind a farm.

Our bear puppets collection was used for tactile teaching the importance of friendship and to increase the children's vocabulary. They engaged their audience in an imaginary adventure trip with interactive storytelling, singing and always put a smile on a child's bright shining face. The referral came from another teacher that had attended our program in the classroom and knew about my peanut heritage. We dropped by for a visit to introduce the program. The librarian, Mrs. Mason, was eager to meet with us to discuss our new cardboard box pop-up mobile on-site classroom program that was getting so much buzz around town. After meeting with her, she showed immediate interest and was most supportive. She opened the doors to the library for the first time for us to offer our program to several childcare centers in and around the city.

We were elated that in the spirit of teamwork, and believing in the vision it could really happen again. But to get the ball rolling, we were asked to *volunteer* our services first so she could get a feel for the flow of the program. There was no doubt about volunteering as I reflected back on the two poems, the heart gifts in my classroom and the words of wisdom.

The interview was so inspiring and she was such an awesome woman, it was our pleasure to help her out. Only this time around, we all yielded major benefits and won the championship. Mrs. Mason agreed to host us and we continued to work together over the years on many occasions with our themed based creative dance movement programs. Fortunately, we had managed to establish a frequent attendance of children that visited the library and a positive work relationship. We are grateful for her keeping her word as we were later faced with a dilemma that changed the direction of our programs.

In an attempt to cancel our upcoming scheduled events in April 2009, she encouraged us to stay focused on recovery leaving the doors open to return later in the year. As the school year rapidly approached, she invited us to return in the fall of 2009. This was to participate in an event that was geared toward learning about the journey of the peanut and how it traveled around the world before coming to Virginia. Surprisingly, that was the invitation that sparked the birth of Penny Peanut's teaching toolbox character.

Due to my limited mobility to perform as a creative dance movement teacher, we redirected our program with a storyline using a variety of teaching styles and large visual board displays in an effort to resume my work. We were deeply appreciative for her support. This was the opportunity which allowed us to continue moving forward using a different approach to get the job done, so we took our huge cardboard box pop-up mobile on-site classroom program and hit the stage again. With new opportunities on the rise, we searched to find creative ways to help convey the message that children could relate to on the visual level to help them learn the importance of the spirit of teamwork.

Penny Peanut's storyline was inspired by my journey of a little peanut girl born on a farm. She was caught up in a major rain storm and needed the help of her friends to get her home. Penny teaches about the journey of the peanut using a P's word map book which helps the children learn to read the signs and follow directions. Their job as a team is to help her return to her hometown for a community event. This was at the Miles B. Carpenter Museum to work with the local children.

After revamping our previous program and using a different style to convey the message, without hesitation, she agreed to host our mobile Life on the Farm Museum. Penny Peanut and Ms. Sunshine hit the stage together for the first time. The message was spreading to others as we continued to grow with our cultural enrichment program that included the historical information displays and the peanut heritage of Sussex County. Her storyline gives them a historic tour on a child's level of her travels and friends from around the world.

Children were able to connect with Penny Peanut easily, and she has been able to teach a number of things. She encourages them to work together to help others. They must do so in the spirit of teamwork as they play and learn about the many foods and animals that grow and live on the farm. She has made it a point to teach her friends about the eight most common foods that causes allergies. They are eggs, fish, milk, soy, peanuts, wheat, shellfish and tree nuts.

Later, we were referred to a second librarian, Mrs. Darden, who gained interest in us and had inquired about programs in the area. Penny Peanut was opening up new doors for us to continue to spread the message, and we welcomed the opportunity. During the interview, she mentioned that there was a buzz in town about a preschool teacher and a professional musician that had developed a thriving interactive story time program. Interestingly, she stated that what caught her attention were the use of various teaching styles with large educational visual display boards that we used to deliver the message. They were designed to bring a unique touch with adventure to the floor when it comes to engaging everyone in the audience. Still somewhat concerned, Mrs. Darden was uncertain because of the preschool children ages and their level of cognitive development.

Now the wheels were finally turning at this point, as we continued to move forward and making progress again with our work. However, this time things were a little different in trying to present our program in this library. In this particular case, we were hitting a few bumps in the road, whereas previously things had been going so smoothly for us. Although we had piqued her interest, she suggested that we *volunteer* our program at the upcoming summer reading kick-off before coming on board. Afterwards, she was elated and interested wanting to pursue this further. She decided to possibly host us for an event for the upcoming school year.

We met later to discuss future plans. At this point the pressure was really on with this interview, but we continued to believe in our work as it piqued her interest more in our programs. Finally, she saw our sheer passion and perseverance. After the interview, Mrs. Darden agreed to host our program in the spirit of teamwork and everyone had a blast. That experience empowered us to keep moving forward with our pop-up box mobile on-site classroom. She even recommended us to other librarians, suggesting that they give us a chance at their stage.

By this time, we are on our third librarian, Mrs. Tunstall. The buzz was still spreading about Penny Peanut's

Program. As we moved forward, it was smooth sailing without any challenges during this interview. Mrs. Tunstall was also a little peanut girl from peanut country. Based on her observation of our previous programs and the referral, she took us right under her wings without any questions. Furthermore, she was a very compassionate woman, sincerely encouraging, who loved the children and her work.

Following our interview, in the spirit of teamwork, she agreed to host us, confirmed the date and was very excited about seeing the mobile *Life on the Farm Museum*. Her encouraging words were to never stop doing the work that we do, and take every chance possible to read to a child. Unfortunately, due to unforeseen circumstances, she encountered a medical emergency and never got to be a part of this program or returned to work.

Sincerely heartbroken, we continued to believe in our work with our pop-up mobile on-site classroom program. In the spirit of teamwork, we picked up the torch and made an attempt to carry it to the finish line for our friend, who was no longer in the race. This led us back to the Main Public Library. This is where everything had started with Mrs. Mason who opened the doors for us but was no longer there.

At this point, we are now on yet another librarian, Ms. Moore. Holding on with hope and after a brief introduction, Ms. Moore immediately agrees to interview us and is very understanding, kind and supportive; so much that she brings in an assistant, Ms. Pollard, to help us plan our program. Upon reviewing our video contents, she went forward with hosting us. In the spirit of teamwork, our plans went so smoothly, it was unbelievable.

Thinking that this is the final deal, Ms. Moore politely asks us to *volunteer* at an upcoming event. This was planned for an out of town author the next week that wanted to introduce her new book. She stated that we had made such a buzz in town with our Penny Peanut Program and her story time, that it would be a good draw to increase attendance.

After years of volunteering to help others, the blessings of continued work opportunities were flowing our way. We gladly agreed to help her out with the introduction of our Can-Do Kids Program. Once again we hit the stage, only this time in full swing and a new future direction.

Penny Peanut performed her last presentation at the Richmond Public Main Library in the Auditorium on February 15, 2012. Some of the children were introduced for the first time to, Ms. Sunshine, the little peanut girl from Waverly, Virginia representing the Nation's First Peanut Museum in U.S.A., where her story started at birth and ends at her home on the farm.

After this amazing experience, we felt the time had finally come for us to say farewell to the stage for a while. In doing so, we loaded up our teaching toolbox characters, the Luv Bear Stars and settled down in the studio.

With new changes on the horizon, and the opportunity to reach a greater audience through the use of modern technology, we decided to put our program in book format. A simple introduction to early learning for anyone to enjoy with a child and activities using your imagination can be found in our first book Luv Bear Stars! Learning is Sunshiny Fun.

Penny Peanut's New Message of Hope

Believe in yourself

The message of hope is to encourage children to believe in themselves as they participate in our Can-Do Kids Program. They can become future stars on the runway of life by learning early skills, developing friendships and working together through the spirit of teamwork. The message is delivered in a storyline when Penny Peanut's character's helper shares with her audience the history of her peanut heritage while growing up in Waverly, Virginia in Sussex County. She along with her friend, Mrs. Y., were among the first commercial early peanut crops grown in the U.S.A in or around 1842 after traveling around the world.

Penny made a promise to her friend, who was also a little peanut girl, that someday she would return and they would plant her one seed of hope together. Through their work, they wanted to make a difference in the lives of others by encouraging community involvement.

Her only dream was to have the courage to make it back home in time for the event and see the Cherry Blossom Trees come into full bloom. It was very important that she came during springtime when the temperatures were warm, so that they could plant it and reap a great fall harvest to share with others.

Penny Peanut's friend helped her plan her special event at the central facility in town. The event is being held at the Miles B. Carpenter Museum. This is where they will meet to play and learn their ABC's while they Read about Seeds. She encouraged them to bring extra seeds with them so that they could plant them in the Friendship Unity Garden in the Community. Afterwards, they will join in the fun of sharing their books at the Book Swap.

Some of her friends had already heard about the nice gentleman, Miles B. Carpenter, she knew while she was growing up back home. He was a longtime resident in the town who had left his home behind to be used as his legacy. He wanted everyone in the community to enjoy it and to be a place for all artists in the region to display their work. She continued to believe in the dream and never gave up hope. In the spirit of teamwork and help from her friends, she finally made it home after an incredible journey.

Faith and Courage

Believe in miracles

It is amazing how I jumped through so many hurdles as I continued to work diligently with my on-site pop-up box themed based programs sharing our heart gifts. You'll soon see the doors opening again, to the point where I was dancing with the children all over the classrooms making learning fun. On the other hand, an unpredicted rain storm was quickly approaching my own pathway. Together with faith, understanding my purpose and the miraculous blessing of recovery gave me the courage to never give up on this dream idea to keep moving forward.

Have you ever thought about what you might encounter as you attempt to work throughout your day? Would you believe that I am also a Professional Joey Clown? The sole purpose of attending clown classes was to bring more creative teaching and engagement to my story time in the classroom.

Upon my arrival at the center, the morning was lovely and the sky was filled with fluffy clouds as the warm spring air was slowly breezing through the trees. Finally, my work schedule was finished for the day from teaching a creative dance movement class. This was on the morning of (Friday, April 3, 2009) at a local learning center. The children all gathered around anxiously awaiting their goodbye hugs and stickers after their program with Clown Luv and The Luv Bears. Before leaving, I stopped in to say goodbye to the Learning Center Director, Mrs. Sheila, who was also the founder of the community based childcare center. She was a very compassionate and empathetic woman who showed a deep concern for everyone. The Learning Center offered an excellent service to many children and their families in the community.

Additionally, this was a non-profit church learning center that had established a long-term working relationship with me in order to provide mobile on-site services for their preschoolers. The children and staff always enjoyed our programs as we all shared many priceless moments working together over the years. Nevertheless, it never crossed my mind that this would be my last goodbye to so many bright little happy smiling faces for an extended period of time.

You'll soon see the connection and my passion for the children in my classroom, as I left them waving goodbye standing at their windows. My heart was filled with joy as I returned home to prepare for a special event back in my hometown. This was the Cherry Blossom Festival in Waverly, Virginia planned for the next day (Saturday, April 4, 2009) at the Miles B. Carpenter Museum. This was an exciting moment for me to see the Cherry Blossom Trees come into full bloom again. We were scheduled on the program to entertain the local children in the area that knew us and were looking forward to our return visit.

There are many ways to try to understand this experience, but for us our faith is what kept us believing in the vision and focusing on a new direction. While preparing for my trip, an unfortunate thing happened, as I encountered a severe bout of pain with a sudden onset of illness. This landed me in a hospital emergency room for the evening. After a battery of tests, they decided to admit me. My primary concern was not for myself, but for the wonderful children coming to my special event back home at the Miles B. Carpenter Museum the next day. I had surgery on the morning of the special event and encountered post-op complications that became life-threatening placing me in the ICU for an extended stay.

After spending over thirty days in the hospital and later in rehabilitation with months of physical therapy, this was a turning point in our lives. For sure, this caused us to redirect our plans, pray and find the peace to calm the storm. Due to the complexity that surrounded the post-op complications, I was left with the inability to walk for a period of time and limited mobility. This restricted me to return to my classroom and work with young children. Therefore, I could not resume my full work schedule as a creative dance movement teacher, and had to put my dancing shoes on the shelf. This was truly an unpredicted life changing rain storm that forced me to think even further outside of the box. Without a doubt, this was unlike the sudden rain storm classroom dilemma that was instantly fixed with a cardboard box.

Understanding the lessons learned by being resilient and embracing the challenge of my obstacles opened the doors to spark a new direction to keep moving forward. With that in mind, having faith, family, friends, believing in the dream idea and the joy of working with the children again gave me the courage to never give up hope.

Consequently, the weekend plans to spend some quality time with the three wise elderly women back home and share a few words of wisdom over a great cup of tea never took place. They are mothers and mentors with loving hearts that stood firmly in the gap delivering messages of hope as they walked along beside us on this miraculous road to recovery. When they got the call, they were deeply saddened and reached out to us with their loving support. Mrs. Hudson called the entire family and they all came with Mrs. Loving, the family minister who immediately gathered everyone around as she kneeled at my bedside holding my hand praying, "She is an extraordinary woman who uses her God given gifts and talents to touch many lives in her daily walk. We are grateful for her spiritual guidance and counsel."

Mrs. Yancey shared her encouraging words of wisdom to continue to be strong and get well while she held the doors open for our safe return home. Mrs. Alston amazed us as she reached out and sent her pastor, Reverend Ross from my hometown to my bedside to offer his spiritual guidance and counsel. He is a great mentor who had opened his doors for us to volunteer our Vacation Bible School Outreach Program to the local children in the community.

    This life changing rain storm was not exactly my cup of tea. But the overflow of the blessings came with the support of the amazing women and men who walked along beside us every step of the way. Again, many people in the spirit of teamwork volunteered their time helping out as we zoned in on the possibilities of a new beginning. Have you ever thought about the kindness in the hearts of people that are observing your potential? There are many that are just waiting to give you a helping hand to get back on your feet.

    Let me tell you about this awesome friendship. While trying to find ways to redirect and return to work, Mrs. Sheila came to my rescue during my recovery. We met for lunch and a walk in the park at the lake and shared ideas. Would you believe that she was the Director of the learning center? She contacted me stating that the children were asking about my return and getting anxious and curious.

    Afterwards, she suggested that I drop by their classroom for a brief visit. This was to reassure them and to calm their fears. To share in their learning at art time, they all created their special little masterpieces. It turned out that they were a bunch of get well cards with their own personal signatures. Included in the packet was a note from her stating that they missed seeing us. They were wondering what happened to their dance teacher, Clown Luv and The Luv Bears that made them smile while they enjoyed learning. You'll be excited to learn that, it was that moment in time and request that sparked a ray of light on it all and started the ball rolling again.

The learning center offered us an open invitation with our programs based on what we felt we could handle. Keeping that door of opportunity open to return was the birth of our first teaching tools box characters. Would you believe this was the best challenge of them all, trying to figure out what to do with a bunch of busy preschoolers in a classroom! Being able to return back to visit their bright little smiling faces was the peace that calmed the rain storm and let the sunshine back into my work.

Suddenly, the green light flashed with another idea. At this point, I was so grateful to be able to walk again that I put my dancing shoes on the shelf. With that in place, we honored their request and dropped in for a brief story time. We returned with our new Luv Bear Stars on Wheels Story Time Program, with a bright yellow apron and a huge Friendship Bear. Ms. Sunshine had personal interactive activity rugs and a large book to read. We gradually added our cardboard box pop-up scenes as we started to rebuild. The children were all happily greeting us and joined in a fun story time. The highlight of the moment came when they wanted to know the name of their new bear friend. I told them that they all could call me Ms. Sunshine with Luv Bear Sunshine now because of the joy of being able to return to their classroom again and seeing their bright little sun shining faces.

In an effort to gradually rebuild our status we contacted everyone to cancel our previously scheduled programs due to the sudden changes we were faced with. In this particular case, an interesting thing happened when we contacted one librarian that had been working with us for a while. We were elated at her response to our request to cancel our program. She kindly encouraged us to stay focused on recovery with the possibility of an invitation for the fall of 2009, not realizing what was hanging in the wind for us on this one. The rest is history and amazing things happened as we kept our minds open to possibly returning.

People that are put in Your Pathway

Keep moving forward

"There is more treasure in books than in all the pirates' loot on Treasure Island." --Walt Disney

While in the process of continuing to look for a new direction as we started to progress in rebuilding the status for our work, we received a referral. Later, I contacted the Director of Services of a local established non-profit reading program in Richmond, Mrs. Jennings. She provided reading services and books to the community to help encourage reading. I explained the situation to her about being involved with an Early Childhood Education Program for a long time, its benefits and my limitations. Mrs. Jennings was an awesome woman that responded positively and immediately supported our cause. But in order for our program to receive books, it had to qualify and meet the standard guidelines and criteria for approval.

Now the real challenges were on for us as we had never had to do this before to get work. My thought was just remember the wise elderly woman with the messages from the two poems and the lessons from the farm. The doors were really swinging open for us as we realized again, that we finally had a green light to pursue our vision for the Literacy Art Reading Program. Eager to keep going, we wanted to see what the possibilities were at this point. To get the ball rolling, we invited Mrs. Jennings to our upcoming program in an effort to gain interest so that her organization would have a better understanding of what we did. She agreed to attend as we presented our Life on the Farm Program with Penny Peanut at the Richmond Public Library in February 2010 to over two hundred children from local childcare centers!

While presenting on stage, my performance was augmented as I looked out into the audience and noticed her interest in the rich historical contents. At this point, I was determined to bring forth a great message in hope of meeting the standard requirements. Mrs. Jennings engaging response to the contents being presented kept me redoubling the performance because we just could not miss out on this deal. It took courage for me to continue on stage with Penny Peanut with my limited mobility issues as this was a true struggle which she observed. We managed to get through the performance and finally made it to the end, with a very positive response from the children and an outstanding review from Mrs. Jennings.

At the closing of the program, she approached the stage to speak with us. She spent some time visiting our informational educational displays. She was a former teacher for over thirty years, and had previously taught history. We were elated as she made her assessment right there on the spot, qualifying our program for approval. The entire farm program including the historical part that surrounded the Miles B. Carpenter Museum and the Nation's First Peanut Museum in U.S.A. had qualified and met the criteria for books. In order for us to move forward on this, she stated that we had to become volunteers. There was an instant flashback to the initial two job experiences. This time there was no question about the spirit of teamwork. This was the first organization that provided books to help us get our Literacy Arts Program started.

We agreed to sign on as volunteers of her program to help with distribution. Being that the time had allowed us to gradually redirect our program by returning to my classroom with Luv Bear Stars on Wheels Story Time, we accepted her invitation. The time finally came for our pop-up huge cardboard box classroom program. We received our first recognition on (Saturday, May 22, 2010) in the "Progress Index" newspaper for participating in the *Life through Literature Festival* as the Luv Bears conducted story time.

This was the beginning of our Book Swap. Outside of distribution of books in my classroom, the first community outreach Book Swap was sponsored by the Miles B. Carpenter Museum during their Summer Camp Luau. Several children attended this exciting event and showed interest in more books than they could carry in their little arms. Immediately, Mrs. West, a dedicated volunteer kindly drove home to get a supply of bags for them to carry their books. Additionally, new doors were opened in the area through the blessings and support of the members, teachers and volunteers of First Baptist Church through their Vacation Bible School Community Outreach. We were truly blessed with a new direction and the abundance of books donated for so many children and their families to help build their home library. Again, as the story continues, it will help you have a better understanding as you gain insight into our work.

Promoting the Peanut Heritage at the State Fair of Virginia

Dream Big

Through the generosity of sponsorships, our company was able to expand the footprint of the museum by displaying our informational and educational program at the State Fair of Virginia. This was combined with a promotional reading kick-off to help encourage reading at home between parents, caregivers and children. The visitors enjoyed the opportunity immensely as they strolled through the displays sharing the history that surrounded the Miles B. Carpenter Museum and the Nation's First Peanut Museum in U.S.A. We were able to capture the interest of thousands of people who stopped by our booth. Brochures were distributed to visitors encouraging them to drop in for a visit to support the museum and the surrounding businesses on their way to the beach.

During our stay, we were able to present a short storyline to young children and their parents that came by to inquire about the farm theme display. The children enjoyed the farm set up, which consisted of a variety of foods that grow on the farm. The miniature animal display included hands-on interactive activities with a hay bale base to help them learn about the various animals and how they live.

Children also participated in a sing-a-long as they learned the ABC's of Reading about Seeds with the Alpha Pals. We distributed a variety of bookmarks donated from our sponsors. They contained positive messages to help children and their parents enjoy fun quality time bonding together while reading. The visitors were able to learn more, through a PowerPoint presentation on the world journey of the peanut, before coming to the USA and Virginia. Again, people from many walks of life were amazed as they learned about the historical landmark and the peanut heritage of Sussex County.

Through our Book Swap we were able to distribute hundreds of mini bags of resource material to help children and their families build their home library. We invited Mrs. Jennings of the reading program to come along and share her experience. We joined together to help promote literacy and bring awareness to the importance of family quality reading time starting at home.

Historic 200 Pound Watermelon Story

The Promise of Two little peanut girls
Enjoy the Little Things

The blessings are still flowing as we are now drinking from our saucer at this point with our new Literacy Arts Program. We were invited to conduct a two day Summer Luau in July 2011, in the backyard of the grounds of the Miles B. Carpenter Museum. Children in the community and from local childcare centers participated. We had a wonderful time as we offered our Book Swap along with a program and storyline of a tour of the Hawaiian Islands. Many other games were provided for the children to enjoy as they played and participated in the activities while sharing at the Book Swap. All of us desired to see the grounds filled with children running, playing, learning and enjoying themselves.

Later, all of the children visiting had an opportunity to share a historical moment with Mrs. Yancey. She told them the true story about the two hundred pound watermelon that was carved by Miles B. Carpenter and the huge sign with a bite that was used as advertisement for his business. Soon after, a local business sent over a supply of cold watermelons and the children all gathered around the tables and enjoyed a delicious snack. The Miles B. Carpenter Museum has supported other programs and has been actively involved in the community in the schools through their sponsorship of cultural enrichment programs. They also serve as a facility that offers art classes, workshops, musical dramas and events for local artists to display their work.

We were invited to return again for a Holiday Program

in the Art Studio in December 2010 to work with children from local childcare centers. The town's youngest artists, ages two and up, created their holiday masterpieces for gifts to give to their love ones. We were asked to return for other Holiday Programs that allowed us to continue to increase the footprint of our Book Swap to local children in the area.

    The Children's Garden at the museum was also maintained by the staff and children in the local childcare center. It was always beautifully decorated and was a great teaching tool for learning about plants, food and nature. Mrs. Ewell, the Director of the childcare center was very supportive during our visits. She always encouraged involvement from others in the community. We deeply appreciate her support along with the other centers and all of the wonderful children that they have allowed us to work with over the years. We have continued to visit events that were planned, but never making it back to see the Cherry Blossom Trees until my mentor, Mrs. Yancey, decided to retire and offer just one more opportunity.

Cherry Blossom Trees and the Volunteer Appreciation Ice Cream Social

Follow your heart

The time finally came, some four years later, for me to get another chance to return home to watch the Cherry Blossom Trees come into full bloom. As previously mentioned earlier, this was at the Volunteer Appreciation Ice Cream Social at the Miles B. Carpenter Museum on April 7, 2013. We all sat around as we enjoyed the museum grounds on a beautiful Sunday afternoon while the soft breezy spring winds sifted through the trees. Many of the attendees were dressed in pink and an array of beautiful spring colors that complimented the scene of the pink blooms on the trees planted around the complex.

In many ways, for me this event touched my heart deeply as the memories flowed and the miraculous recovery journey in an attempt to attend this event four years ago. It was truly an inspiration to know that I was always welcome back home and had a place to display my work. The welcome message was delivered by Museum President, Mrs. Yancey.

One of the most remarkable facts came about as I observed her speech. In my view, I saw an extraordinary wise elderly woman of courage and strength that had traveled an incredible journey, volunteering for twenty eight years. She had come to a place where she was now passing the torch on to someone else to continue the legacy of Miles B. Carpenter. Her wisdom truly exemplified the message, as she shared memories and acknowledged the support of many volunteers and supporters that had dedicated their hearts and time. We all sat back as she recognized the spirit of teamwork initially with the original group of volunteers. In addition, she acknowledged the support of all of the volunteers and their dedication as being the foundation for the success of the museum. This was truly a genuinely passionate, heartfelt message of hope that could be seen through her loyalty and work over the last twenty eight years.

While looking out over the grounds, I observed many people from all walks of life that have come together to enjoy and share in this special moment of fellowship. All in all, the grounds were packed full of volunteers that had accepted an invitation to support their community and went forth with their dream ideas as well. I glanced around as I watched volunteers with their cameras still capturing pictures of historical, cultural and charitable events that were promoted by the museum. One in particular, was Ms. Lee, who is truly dedicated to the camera for the museum and has been a longtime volunteer. Many artists and presenters in the community and around the region have gathered at this central facility and found it to be a home place to display their unique work.

This is a story of courage that teaches even in the midst of a horrific rain storm of thunder, lighting, wind and rain, with hope you can still find the sunshine in the clouds. Since that time, in an effort to continue our work, several family members, friends and organizations have reached out to help us continue our cause. That is truly how the real life story unfolded for the two little peanut girls. They ended up right back in their native town at a Volunteer Ice Cream Social still spreading the message of hope and planting seeds in their community. We continued to move forward throughout the summer, as the fall rapidly approached while we prepared for our upcoming school year programs.

After settling down and volunteering for the museum,

we were once again invited to the annual Peanut Harvest Time back home, which we have always looked forward to attending. The exciting thing this time is that Mrs. Y and Penny Peanut will return home together to visit the children in the community with the M&M WOW-MOMS TEAM. They are the three wise elderly women that were waiting back home to share a few words of wisdom with me over a great cup of tea in April 2009. Currently, they are role model teaching toolbox characters in books for our Can-Do Kids Program.

Peanut Harvest Time
November 2, 2013
Return Home to Visit

Show Gratitude

The grounds were quickly filling up as exhibitors arrived to set up their displays all around the Miles B. Carpenter Museum Complex.

As always, many dedicated volunteers were teaming up, doing what their hearts have always done, giving a helping hand. The beautiful scenery was all too consuming as the early fall morning evolved into a warm sunny day while music echoed in the air. Today, some fifteen years later, we are still returning home to attend the Peanut Harvest Time as we continue to spread the message through our mobile educational displays.

Once again, we were warmly welcomed by the newly appointed Museum Administrator, Mr. Roane, volunteers and supporters in and around the community. Additionally, our special place was all ready to go for setting up the presentations. So many wonderful people came by to visit while we set up. It is heartfelt moments such as these that you relish when you feel a sincere welcome back to your home community.

Meanwhile, children that attended had fun playing, running, jumping and enjoying the animals at the petting farm. Many families and children joined us in a storyline, videos, and PowerPoint presentation while learning about the museum and the peanut heritage. The scenery was beautiful and new attractions were available as the attendees visiting enjoyed themselves immensely while the volunteers continued to give their support.

Our programs have expanded over the years with our cardboard box displays. They have been designed as a mobile pop-up on-site classroom museum for educational purposes. New displays for young children were designed around our *Life on the Farm* Program through a variety of pictures of a Fair Exhibition to help encourage fun while being involved with interactive learning. In particular, this scene was selected in an effort to help make learning the journey of peanuts fun through hunting for peanut facts at the World Fair. The information included in the mini displays for children is a brief introduction to help gain knowledge about peanuts and a variety of other foods that grow on the farm.

It also gives a little history about peanuts and their travels around the world. Penny Peanut is a teaching toolbox character that brings other messages such as Read about Seeds and the eight most common foods that cause allergies. They also learn about the many nutritional benefits of peanuts as well as peanut butter and the many ways to use them. Displays for older children and adults were designed to help bring knowledge of the many aspects that surround the peanut history and the historical landmark that commemorates the early planting of peanut crop in or around 1842 in Sussex County.

They were presented on a level that both adults and children could relate. This is done in an effort to help increase awareness of agriculture education and preserve the historical peanut heritage. Two of our teaching toolbox characters came along with their friends this time to help with the program. We were delighted to have Mrs. Y's real life character, Mrs. Yancey join us in a surprise visit to give us some brief comments and a few words of wisdom for our children. She left a superb video message on school success and continued learning for our Can-Do Kids.

Mrs. Y's character will continue on with us in our future program. She, along with many others are, part of our M&M WOW-MOMS (Mothers and Mentors with Words of Wisdom and Mothers of Multiple Skills) TEAM. This is a new addition to our existing program to help share a few encouraging words. Our hope is that the children will reap the benefits from the positive role models that have traveled incredible journeys in their lives. Their teachings are many as they encourage you not to dwell on what you can't do, but what you can. Keep believing in the dream and don't sweat the small stuff.

All in all, this is a message of hope that two little peanut girls truly believed, that their dream idea could become reality through their spirit of teamwork. We deeply appreciate all of the years that we have shared with so many wonderful people. As we move forward, Penny Peanut, Mrs. Y and Ms. Sunshine will continue to share the messages of hope. The M&M WOW-MOMS TEAM will also continue to encourage others through their words of wisdom and poems. In summary, accept the invitation when someone invites you to volunteer in your community for one day. In the spirit of teamwork, it will yield many blessings to others that come into your pathway.

With your support you can plant future seeds of hope, fill many cups that will overflow and you truly will drink from your saucer. Keep the faith, have the courage to move forward on your vision, even if there is no pay. Finally, embrace the words of wisdom, never give up and do it anyway.

A Special Thank You to Miles B. Carpenter Museum

Discover your passion

While growing up in my hometown, I had the pleasure of knowing Miles B. Carpenter. Our family would stop by his roadside stand and ice house to purchase items from him. He was a very pleasant and friendly gentleman, especially to children. One of the interesting things about him was the pleasure that he found as he enjoyed making all of us laugh at his statues in the back of his Chevrolet Truck. Just in the same way, he would always smile while looking at our puzzled faces left in wonderment as we tried to figure out the mystery behind the moving wood people. Later, we all discovered that he had designed them to move their arms and other body parts.

At a young age, my most treasured memory of all was the lady that rode around town in the front seat with him. On the other hand, as I continued my work and research into this project, I began to fully understand the meaningful purpose and his reason behind it all. Even though, many years passed we continued to watch him drive by with the lady always in the front seat.

Despite the fact that she never waved back to us while we played outside, we were expected to still use our nice manners. As it happened, we just listened, did it anyway and kept on waving to her. As young children and simply being curious, we began to wonder that it was rather odd as we did not understand why she did not wave back or turn to look at us. Just think how it felt when the opportunity presented itself one day as the truck drove into the driveway to deliver ice. Our moment in time came as the passenger side faced us while we played outside. This was our chance for a close-up view as we quickly walked over and spoke to her. Interestingly, she did not wave back or speak, and simply did not move at all. What is clear is that, we finally got it as it dawned on us that she was not a real person, neither were the carved people in the back of his truck. Subsequently, this was his unique style of work as a Folk Artist, wood carver and a way of advertising his business.

  In conclusion, a special thank you from the little peanut girl, who finally made it back home that spring to plant her seed of hope and to reap a great fall harvest that will last a lifetime. The heart gift that he left behind has made memories for us of a lifetime to enjoy upon returning home. Who could ever forget a great Folk Artist and our town ice man that left a heart gift behind such as this for everyone to enjoy in the community? This incredible journey has touched my heart deeply as it has embarked hope in the future to continue to plant seeds of hope through our programs. I am delighted to have had the pleasure of sharing our story and am thankful for the trails of people on our pathway and their encouraging words. My hope is that everyone has gained more insight and knowledge as to how this series of events came about. It is amazing what can happen when someone reaches out and invites you to a community event to volunteer. You might just leave a little trail of heart gifts behind that will make memories of a lifetime!

www.ingramcontent.com/pod-product-compliance
Lightning Source LLC
Chambersburg PA
CBHW061248040426
42444CB00010B/2291